social·ish

A FAIL PROOF GUIDE TO RELATIONSHIPS

jason scales

ISBN: 978-1-6553348-8-7
ISBN: 978-1-6553348-8-7 (eBook)

Cover Design: Glenn Schumpert of Crown'D
(www.crowndbrand.com) Brentwood, Tennessee USA

Design & Layout: Michael Matulka of Basik Studios
(www.gobasik.com) Omaha, Nebraska USA

Printed in the United States of America

10 9 8 7 6 5 4 3 2 1

social·*ish*

INTRODUCTION
social · *ish*

During a conversation with a young member of my family, something was said that caught me off guard. We were discussing how people interact with one another, and she unexpectedly blurted out, "I don't do people."

What she meant by this statement is she doesn't like being around other people, she prefers not to interact with others, and she tries to avoid relationships altogether. This shocked me because she always flourishes around people and appears to be a social butterfly.

My family member's statement made me think of all the times I have heard people say similar things, but I paid it no attention. However, the truth is – for various reasons – some people excel at interacting with others, and some people simply...don't.

Regardless if you're a life-of-the-party extrovert, or a loner who prefers being a homebody, it's impossible to avoid having relationships in this world.

I believe that life is not meant to be lived alone and relationships are essential for achieving life's greatest goals. To accomplish these goals, I believe we must continuously strive to improve and perfect our interactions with one another.

To that point, I have developed a concept called being "social-ish," which is an understanding that we all need to possess certain qualities and characteristics that will help us connect with other people.

The word "social" means needing companionship and therefore being best suited to living in communities.

The word "ish" means having the qualities or characteristics of.

To be social-ish means regardless of your intrinsic introverted or extroverted nature, you have a love from God that teaches you how to interact with others in a way that can benefit you, your neighbor, your community and can ultimately positively change the world.

My Journey to Being Social-*ish*

I am introverted by nature and struggled for years with relationships. I have blamed all kinds of things for this. For a long time, I thought it was simply just my personality, or possibly a product of my ethnic background and upbringing. I've even blamed other people for my inability to connect with others. Of the many anti-social experiences I have had in my life, I'll share one story with you.

In my 20s, I worked as a financial underwriter. We frequently traveled for work, and one night my co-workers and I ended a long day at a restaurant in Dallas, Texas. The restaurant was packed, and everyone was having a good time; everyone except me. I sat in a section of the restaurant by myself watching basketball. Dressed in a suit and drinking Dr. Pepper, I'm sure I looked lonely and miserable to anyone who casually observed me.

My boss asked if I was ok, and of course I said "yes." But I internally asked myself the same question; "Why was I sitting alone?" One reason I told myself is because, *"I was raised in church and I don't drink alcohol. So, while others are unwinding with adult beverages, my salvation and anointing set me apart and prevent me from joining my colleagues. That's why I don't mesh."*

In reality, I couldn't have been more WRONG! There were plenty of other Christians in the group who were having a good time.

The truth is, I didn't know how to connect.

I didn't know how to find commonalties with people outside of my comfort zone. My comfort zone included my friends from church, family members and close acquaintances. If a person didn't fall into one of those three categories, then it was very difficult for me to let them into my world.

Eventually, my inability to relate to others began to impact my job performance. A part of my job was not just knowing how to crunch numbers, but it also involved connecting with people and forming relationships. I was being overlooked for promotions and missing other opportunities because I didn't know how to open up. I got tired of feeling left out, hanging by myself and missing "home," the only place I felt comfortable.

I struggled with this for years, and I knew I had to take a different approach to relationships.

Everything changed for me when I met a man who read my personality like a book and showed me how to write a new story for myself. He taught me practical steps I could take to begin connecting with people more easily. He was very successful in his career and I guess that's what made me listen to him.

This gentleman showed me a model for analyzing the various types of relationships I have and how to approach each one accordingly. This model changed my perspective, and I started to embrace my own personality as well as people from all walks of life. I learned that every soul is full of potential, and if we can get out of our own way, we can do remarkable things in life together.

I am not perfect, and I sometimes fail at relationships. But at least now I have principles to reference to help me get through the challenges I face.

You may identify with being a classic introvert or you may be on the opposite end of the spectrum. Maybe your extroverted self doesn't meet a stranger and you have a plethora of amazing friends. Regardless of your personality type or experiences in life, we all have a common longing to connect, belong and engage with one another.

Throughout this book, I will share the things I've learned about setting a firm foundation for new, existing and future relationships. And then, I'll discuss how to properly engage and interact within each relationship in order to receive maximum benefits.

The Social-*ish* Model

The social-ish model is the basis of this entire book. Before we get started with the model, let's first go over a few definitions:

- **Relationship** – The way in which two individuals or parties are established with each other that determine how they interact with each other

  Examples: Parents and children, husband and wife, employee and employer, friends, associates, coach and players, mankind and God

- **Engagement** – How parties in a relationship interact with each other to produce benefits

Examples: Communication, planning, praying, praising, complimenting, helping

- **Benefits** – Results of healthy engagement within a relationship

  Examples: Safety, protection, success, happiness, comfort, sex, championships, revolution, innovation.

In summary, here's how the relationship model works.

To receive the benefits of a relationship, you must engage and interact properly within that relationship.

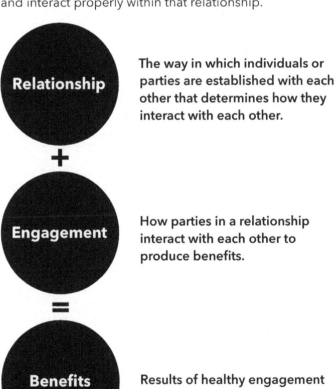

Relationship — The way in which individuals or parties are established with each other that determines how they interact with each other.

Engagement — How parties in a relationship interact with each other to produce benefits.

Benefits — Results of healthy engagement within a relationship.

I know. It's too simple, right? You probably went back and read it again and asked yourself, "what did I miss?" However, I have learned that many times the simplest ideas – when practiced with discipline and diligence – can produce the greatest rewards.

If you are not seeing benefits and rewards from a relationship, then that's an indication that something is wrong. Maybe you're not interacting properly. Or maybe you're engaging with the wrong people in the wrong way. Throughout this book, we'll examine in detail the methods for identifying the reasons why relationships suffer and what to do to bring them back to a healthy state.

Connecting with each other can be challenging because mankind is loaded with purpose, potential, personalities, and unfortunately... problems. However, if we can tear down the artificial walls, we've built to protect our hearts and embrace great people in the right manner, then we can receive the many rewards of positive relationships and accomplish tremendous things in life.

As we study the social-ish relationship model, we will learn techniques to enhance our ability to do just that.

social·*ish*

social·*ish*
TABLE OF CONTENT

social·*ish*

CHAPTER 1
How to be social·*ish*?

Create Relationship "Safe Zones"

I recently joined a gym that has a mission to create an environment where people of all fitness levels can feel like they belong. To accomplish this culture of inclusiveness, there are big signs on the wall that say things like, "No Judgement Zone," and "You Belong Here." The athletic trainers and gym employees don't make you feel horrible and condemn you for being in poor physical shape. Instead, their goal is to lift you up to the fitness level you desire.

These ideals struck my heart and I thought *"this is how relationships should be."*

Every relationship in your life should be based in love and exist in a safe place free from judgement, shame and criticism. I believe these "safe zones" are a key component to living a social-ish life.

Deep down inside, we all want and need relationships, but many of us avoid connecting with others because we are afraid of being judged. And, like joining a gym, sometimes a desire to be better, a willingness to work hard, and proper engagement of equipment and technique is not always enough to produce the life-changing results we seek. Sometimes the "X" factor that makes successful outcomes possible is simply creating a safe place, a home, and a shelter for these actions to take their full effect.

When we create these safe places for our relationships where we can let our guards down and feel a sense of belonging, then we can learn to love and interact as our authentic selves. Removing barriers around our hearts allows us to welcome in the people and great experiences that God has intended for us. We are then in position to bless people and the world around us.

Being social-ish requires a judgement-free zone for us to develop meaningful relationships and produce positive benefits. So, if we want relationships without judgement and criticism, then does that mean anything goes? There are no rules and all behavior is acceptable? Absolutely not.

Then how do we go about setting standards and creating these safe zones for our relationships?

I believe the building blocks that create these relationship safe zones are agreement, roles and responsibilities, and expectations. The next part of this chapter will walk through each of these concepts and then provide an opportunity for you to complete question and answer checkpoints to evaluate where you stand on each subject.

Seek Agreement in How the Parties Are Established With One Another

The first part of the 3-part social-ish model addresses how individuals or multiple parties are established with one another to form a relationship. This concept happens through coming into agreement with one another.

Countless books have been written, seminars attended, and training manuals purchased to teach individuals how to come into agreement to accomplish a common goal. Those who have managed to successfully do this throughout history have produced phenomenal results.

From Apple revolutionizing communication with the iPhone, to Microsoft's advent of computer software, or even the 1990s Chicago Bulls inspiring basketball dynasty. Many institutions have mastered the art of creating a culture where they operate in agreement to achieve success.

A critical component for arriving at a place of agreement in relationships is establishing a vision that all parties can work together to accomplish. A common challenge is when individuals come together in a relationship and they both have different expectations of what the relationship should look like and produce.

For example, if you ask the average married couple what their idea of a happy marriage is or what one expects from his or her spouse, each spouse normally gives a different answer. If you walk the halls of a small business and ask a manager what his expectations are of the employees who report to him, then you might receive a different response than if you had asked the employee.

So, what brings two or more people together so that they are on the same page as they work toward a common goal? Let's consider some examples of how this happens.

Two individuals who marry are brought together through marriage vows, agreed upon roles and responsibility, and love. Employees and employers come into agreement through job descriptions, an employee manual, a company vision statement and recited values. Two partners in a limited liability corporation form an operating agreement – legal documents that are often required to conduct simple tasks like opening a business back account – to designate roles in which they will play in a company. Members of a sports team paint their mission statement on the locker room wall where coaches, captains, players, reporters, visitors and anyone else who enters can see it.

I have a nephew who loves Legos. It is an absolute joy to watch him take thousands of pieces of plastic of various shapes, colors, and sizes and simply follow instructions to construct a live replica of the picture that's printed on the front of the Lego box. This is a simple illustration of how agreeing on what the result should be and following directions on how to interact with one another can produce the things we seek.

You get the picture. Agreement does not occur by happenstance.

The process of formulating an agreement answers the question, "why did we come together in the first place?" The process is full of joy - and unfortunately sometimes pain -, and many relationships often are dead on arrival after this process.

Reaching a state of agreement is not for the faint of heart, but those who master this critical first step can create tremendous relationships and experiences. If each party is sold on the idea that we can all do more together than we can individually, then this principle turns into the driving force of what leads to compromise and a blending of expectations into one vision that benefits everyone involved.

This Bible scripture affirms that being in agreement is powerful.

Matthew 18:19 states, "Again I say to you, that if two of you agree on earth about anything that they may ask, it shall be done for them by My Father who is in heaven. 20 For where two or three have gathered together in My name, I am there in their midst."

In this passage, we see that:

Relationship = "two of you"

Engagement = "agree on earth about anything they may ask"

Benefit = "it will be done for them by My Father"

I believe every God-ordained relationship has the backing of heaven and is loaded with benefits. What people can do in a relationship is limitless when God is in its midst. And when agreement happens, nothing the relationship sets out to accomplish will be impossible.

Now that we understand the importance of agreement, what is the first step we must take to accomplish it?

Define Roles and Responsibilities

To establish a place of agreement, every relationship must have roles and responsibilities which lead to healthy expectations. A role describes who a person "is" in the relationship. Responsibilities are what a person is supposed to "do" as a result of their role in the relationship.

I know this idea may sound like a boring job description, but unfortunately, I've learned the hard way that an absence of these things is a recipe for disaster.

Consider this story: Peter was raised as an only child and he was the apple of his mother's eye. His mother did everything for him - washed and ironed his clothes, fixed his plate at dinner time, and even bailed him out of financial troubles. Unintentionally, Peter's mother created a monster and Peter became a spoiled brat who relies on his mom for everything.

When Peter marries Judy, he expects Judy to do the same things that his mother had always done.

5

Judy, however, is looking for a life partner. She seeks a husband who is a protector, a provider, is proactive and assertive. Peter refuses to be any of these things because he doesn't feel they are a part of his role. Judy grows frustrated over time and her relationship with Peter grows more contentious with every passing day.

The couple agrees to consult a marriage counselor who, on their first visit, instructs the couple to write down what each other's roles and responsibilities should be. When the counselor presents to Peter her recommendations of a husband's responsibilities towards his wife, Peter is offended. He feels the counselor is siding with his wife and refuses to comply.

Then the counselor makes a statement that shakes Peter to his core.

"Peter, it seems like you are looking for a mother and not a wife," she said.

Peter's eyes were finally opened, and he decided to mature and except his role as a husband.

To avoid this type of confusion, people must first bring definition to their relationships, determine in advance the roles and responsibilities each party agrees to, and make a commitment to submit to their respective roles.

In a world where people shy away from titles and definitions and just want things to flow and be fluid, ambiguity in the area of roles and responsibilities can be detrimental to any effort.

Another short story that demonstrates this idea involves a talented group of neighbors who worked together to repair a park in a local community. They were all excited about the project, they pooled their resources and they collaborated to get the job done. They arbitrarily divided up tasks and quickly completed the park repairs. Because of their initial success, the community asked the same group to conduct ongoing management of the newly rebuilt park.

At the start of the park management project, the neighbors resisted the notion of formally organizing and assigning titles in the group. They had already worked so well together, and they didn't want to ruin a good thing. Eventually, the neighbors lost momentum as tasks began to mount up, they started to butt heads regarding the project's direction and whose ideas and leadership to follow. At the end of the day, it just wasn't fun for them anymore.

They almost disbanded until one of the group members recommended that they organize and determine how each person should contribute to the park management efforts.

The group elected a team leader who served as the ongoing project manager and who also assigned roles and responsibilities according to everyone's strengths. The project manager appointed an architect who monitored the park's infrastructure, a landscaper who maintained the park grounds, and a park ranger who was responsible for communicating with and regulating park visitors.

These assignments completely revived the group and generated greater productivity, creativity and ideas. When there was no definition to the relationship there was no unifying. Why? Because, talent was not being best positioned, people were feeling slighted, and they were relying purely on passion and good faith to get things done.

The assignment of roles and responsibilities was the much-needed course correction to keep the group together.

 **Checkpoint:**

- Have we clearly defined our roles and responsibilities in this relationship so that we both know what to expect from each other? This helps because when problems arise, we can reference our agreement and not resort to our feelings!

Understand Expectations

Managing expectations is a natural by-product of operating in agreement with one another. If you skip the agreement phase, the process of setting and managing expectations is bond to have flaws.

In an ideal relationship, you should be able to ask each party what their expectations are for each other and they both name the same things. Unfortunately, many times, this is not the case. This results in two parties who respect each other becoming frustrated because neither really knows what the other wants, and they both have expectations that are not being met.

You may be thinking *"this is very elementary, what's the point?"* However, if you examine your relationships and those around you, how many people are disappointed and hurt because their relationship expectations are not being met? In a great deal of those relationships, there was no agreement on the front end and an expectation is being placed on a person who cannot produce what is being expected.

Here's a short story to illustrate that point.

A young man is on the basketball team at his school. He thinks the world of his coach, and often tells people the coach is a father-figure to him. The young man's biological father never comes to his games and is generally not a part of the young man's life.

The coach, however, has his own family and has close relationships with all his players. His energy is divided between home, work and coaching, and he does not give any single player special treatment or more attention than the other.

Over time, the young man feels rejected by the coach who he "feels" doesn't spend enough quality time with him, bestow fatherly love or attempt to nurture their relationship much at all. His emotions began to impact his play enough for the coach to notice and pull the young man aside.

"I've noticed you're not yourself lately," the coach said. "What's going on? Is everything ok at home?"

"Honestly, no, everything is not ok," the young man responds. "I've been hoping for a better relationship between you and me, but it's just not happening."

The young man tells the coach that he's deeply hurt because the one person he looked up to like a father didn't seem to care for him more than any other player on the team. The coach explained he had limited capacity to be his father, but he could be the best coach and mentor he could to the young man.

Although their conversation saved the relationship and the young man's play returned to peak level, this is a perfect example of how wires can unknowingly get crossed between two people. The coach in this scenario had little chance of being successful in meeting the young man's expectations because he was completely unaware of what was being expected from him. The young man was not looking for a coach and mentor; he was looking for a father which the coach could not be to him. The coach had no idea the young man was seeking a father figure.

Many relationship problems stem from unrealistic expectations. For example, a girlfriend may expect "husband-type" benefits such as financial stability, safety and security, and other support from her boyfriend that he is not equipped or willing to provide. Or some women may subconsciously place demands on the men in their lives to be a father figure, unknowingly trying to compensate for an absentee father they longed for all their life. On the flip side of the coin, some men place an unfair expectation on their spouses to be both their wife and mother, simultaneously seeking to be reassured and pampered, looking for the mother he never had.

It can be heartbreaking to seek acceptance and approval from a group or individual who does not provide such benefits (either because they are ill-equipped or simply refuse to do so). For instance, a father who refuses to provide for his children, a spouse who is oblivious to the needs of her mate, or a person who is selfish and only thinks of himself. This can result in a person feeling rejected, neglected, used and abused.

But a careful assessment of roles and responsibilities, and frank conversations about expectations at the beginning of a relationship can mitigate some of the risks of people getting hurt. Can I expect you to be who you say you are and to fulfill the duties of your role? When the answer to that question is yes, at that point, I will know it is safe to be in a relationship with you.

 **Checkpoint:**

- Are my expectations of this relationship in line with who this person is to me?

- Can this person I am in relationship with produce the benefits they are supposed to produce?

Understand The Four P's Of Engagement

The second component of the social-ish model is understanding the rules of engagement. In every relationship we must interact appropriately to get the benefits from that relationship. Yes, it can be a task, but when you learn how to do it, I promise it's worth it.

One of the greatest temptations in relationships is to treat people how they treat you or according to how they act. I have learned that following that method will not get you what you want from relationships. Instead, you must treat people according to what you want to see come out of the relationship.

Engagement is an art that comes from the heart, but there is definitely a method to the madness. A part of learning the art is developing an intimate understanding of those with whom you are in relationship so that you can interact with them appropriately.

There are four factors I want you to consider as you engage within your relationships. I call them The Four Ps.

Purpose: a person's reason for existence. Everyone has a "why." This is what drives people, gets their wheels turning, motivates them, and is what people live for. Knowing a person's purpose is important because you will know what appeals to them, how to relate to them, and most important how to help them see fulfillment in life.

Potential: a person's gifts, talents and abilities. This is important to know how to use a person in your life. Don't let that word "use" scare you off. Everyone is afraid of being used when in reality you want people to use you. However, you don't want people to abuse you. Abuse is abnormal use. Use is when you engage a person appropriately according to what they can do. Your job uses you; your kids use you; your church uses you. And all of that is okay because you were designed by God to be used. No one obtains anything of worth and doesn't use it. You just don't want to be taken advantage of and abused.

Personality: how a person expresses himself or herself. I think what makes the world beautiful is not just how people look on the outside but the wonderful ways we express ourselves according to how God made us. Our personalities can be outgoing, reserved, analytical, caring, and the list goes on and on. You must learn people's temperament, their hot buttons, etc, so that you can know how they are wired and what to expect from them in certain situations.

Problems: a person's issues (whether they are innate or self-inflicted). A scripture in the book of Job in the Bible says, "Man that is born of a few days is full of trouble." We have issues we struggle with and then we have habits that we form through personal decisions that we make. Your issues choose you, but you choose your habits. In many relationships, people with problems get into them and they blame the relationships for their personal problems. The relationship is not the problem at all. The problem is they don't take ownership for their personal problems and they project them onto the relationship.

Once you learn The Four Ps about the people you are in relationship with, you can shape your interactions with them wisely to get the benefits from the relationship. When you interact with people, remember every person brings a purpose, potential, personality, and problems to the situation. You must be aware of all of them to be effective with the person. When you operate in grace and love you are not intimidated by anyone's gifts nor are you run off by their issues!

Realize Benefits

The third and most rewarding part of the social-ish model is relationship benefits! Benefits are what make relationships worth the work. A benefit is literally an advantage or profit gained from something.

I love watching the NCAA tournament every year. For me, it's not just about who wins the trophy. It is about watching the laughs, smiles, hugs and camaraderie that's demonstrated when a great team culture exists. I love to hear players refer to their teammates as family and to see people buy into the culture of the program and trust their coaches. So, while many teams will never win a championship trophy, they have been the beneficiaries of an environment where people believe in each other, feel supported, and have a reason greater than their own ambition to work hard.

These same types of benefits are in romantic relationships, work relationships, churches and friendships. Let's talk about some specific benefits produced through engagement in healthy relationships.

Success: Success is the culmination of all your hard work and the accomplishment of your goals. It can manifest itself in many ways and is typically considered a relative term. Some people may quantify success by the amount of money in your bank account, or the number of awards you've won, or the square footage of your home.

I believe that you have achieved success when you can benefit yourself and those around you. For example: when a husband and wife build a successful family, they leave a legacy to their children, grandchildren and all their descendants. And mentors at a community center are successful when they share their wisdom and experience with neighborhood youth who grow up to be community and business leaders. A team of research scientists revolutionize the world with they work together to successfully develop a vaccine for one of the deadliest viruses on the planet.

Success is a powerful, tangible benefit that produces a universal feeling of satisfaction and fulfillment.

Support System: There is no feeling like knowing people have your back and genuinely support you. In the Bible, Jesus can be found explaining his heavenly support system to Peter. When Peter drew his sword to cut off a man's ear in defense of Jesus, He corrected Peter and told him of His divine support system. Matthew 26: 52 states "Then Jesus said to him, 'Put your sword back in its place; for all those who habitually draw the sword will die by the sword. 53 Do you think that I cannot appeal to My Father, and He will immediately provide Me with more than twelve legions of angels?'"

Jesus essentially told Peter, 'I roll deep! I get help and support you don't even know about. I am not alone.'

We operate so much better knowing that we don't have to be on the defense all the time. Another benefit of relationships is protection, safety, support and covering.

This is what parents provide for their children, spouses provide for each other, employers provide for employees, leaders provide for those they lead. It feels good to know that you are not alone.

Sex: Yes! One of the benefits of a marriage relationship between a man and a woman is sex. Sex is not a dirty thing. Sometimes churches portray sex and money as two dirty words that God reluctantly tolerates. They aren't! He created them and in the right place they are blessings. If abused, however, they can create so much disaster. Sex is beautiful and it can produce children and pleasure. It is one of the greatest benefits of marriage. The challenge is many people want this benefit without committing to a marriage relationship.

Synergy: Synergy is broadly defined as the combined effects of two or more organisms to produce a greater result than each would achieve individually. Synergy usually arises when two persons with different complementary skills cooperate. In general, the most common reason why people interact is that it creates synergy.

You see the benefits of synergy and collaboration all around you every day from music, to sports, to business, to media, and even church. Synergy yields beautiful results, but it takes a purposeful effort of gifted and talented individuals to buy into something bigger than themselves.

This is not an all-inclusive list of benefits, and I am sure you can think of many more. What are other benefits that make relationships worth all the hard work even when you feel like quitting, like things are pointless, or you are tempted to be selfish?

Now that we know "how" to be social-ish, let's talk about what happens when we have problems executing these principles. What happens when it's easier said than done, our relationships get out of calibration and we start heading in the wrong direction?

CHAPTER 2

What's the real social · *ish* problem?

Have you ever said, "I'm in a horrible relationship; I need to find a better one"? Or maybe you've heard someone say, "I want a better marriage," "my friends don't understand me," "my boss treats me unfairly," or "I want a better relationship with God,"

If you dig deeper, what is really being said is, "I am not seeing the benefits from my relationships."

If I say I want a better marriage, what I am really saying is I do not feel synergy with my spouse, my spouse is not providing a strong support system for me, or I am lacking some other important benefit from my marriage.

If I say I need a better relationship with God, what I'm really saying is I feel like God is not answering my prayers, I am not seeing the favor or blessing of God in my life, or I feel empty like God is not with me.

The deeper questions you should be asking yourself are: *Am I communicating and checking in regularly with my spouse to cultivate a strong marriage? Am I displaying care towards my spouse? Am I praying and reading my Bible to draw closer to God? Am I worshipping and praising Him?*

The answer to the latter questions is probably "no" because maybe you feel like it wouldn't save the marriage, or maybe you feel that God is not listening. Every healthy relationship should produce benefits, but it is impossible to see the benefits of God or human relationships if you do not engage in them.

What do people do when they start to feel distant from each other? They stop communicating, they pull away and they take a break. When people start to have engagement problems, they become disengaged, they stop interacting with others and they retreat to a very guarded place. Maybe they sit alone in a corner of a restaurant instead of joining their colleagues for dinner and drinks. Or maybe they stop going to church and visiting the sick. Married people begin to say, "I don't feel it anymore, we aren't on the same page. I feel like we have grown apart," and they stop confiding in their spouses.

This is how engagement in relationships starts to break down. Many times, when relationships reach this crossroad, instead of repairing what has gone wrong, the parties involved begin searching for a way out. An escape route. An exit ramp. The path of least resistance to get away from their troubled associations.

The truth is, many people have great relationships and most issues can be resolved. If everyone is willing to put in the work, the bonds between two parties can be salvaged, restored and returned to a flourishing state.

Understanding Engagement Problems

In Chapter 1, we discussed how detrimental unfair expectations, lack of definition and unwillingness to comply with role responsibilities can be to relationships. These are common catalysts for relationship failure. Working through the Q&A checkpoints in Chapter 1 should help you identify if those are your issues.

Many relationships, however, break down in the engagement phase. In this chapter, we'll explore how to identify engagement problems, discuss how to fix them, or when to consider potentially making the decision to move on and leave the broken relationship behind. If you can't identify your problems, your relationship could be doomed. Or you may stay in a relationship that you need to walk away from!

Successful engagement is the way to obtain benefits out of relationships. When this component of the social-ish model is out of balance, there will be no benefits. Let's look at some challenges people have regarding engagement.

Many challenges in relationships happen because people project their own insecurities and shortcomings onto the other parties. They blame the relationship or the other person in the relationship for their personal problems.

Let me give you an example.

Jason gets a job at XYZ company. Jason is a smart and likeable guy. He catches on well and is a fast learner. His only challenge is he procrastinates since he knows he can figure anything out and tells himself he works better under pressure. He also tends to over think things and overreact instead of stilling himself and asking questions for a full understanding.

Jason loves his job at XYZ company. He always checks his email late at night. One night, his boss emails him and requests a meeting with him first thing in the morning. Jason doesn't sleep that night thinking of all the reasons why his boss might want to meet. The next morning, Jason is worked up and goes into the meeting defensive and on guard against any potential accusation. His boss starts the meeting with positive feedback.

"Jason, you're a great employee," she begins. "We love having you here, and we think you have a great future with the company." She continued, "but we have some concerns and would like for you to have some additional training."

What Jason interpreted was different from what was actually said. He heard, *"You are about to be fired and this training program idea is just for legal purposes to justify what we are about to do!"*

Jason attends the required training, but he doesn't engage. He starts applying for other jobs, and second guesses himself. Internally, he knows he needs to get a grip, but he doesn't.

He begins to project his internal issues onto everyone he works with: the trainer, coworkers, his boss, the cafeteria lady, and the janitor. His boss notices the change and pulls him to the side. She is a good leader, so she gets to the core of his challenges. She tells him she went through the same thing and that is why she recommended he get additional training because it helped her.

Jason feels horrible because he finally gets a grip, listens to his boss, and he gets back on track. His job performance and his relationship with his colleagues suffered because he didn't know how to engage with them. He didn't have a job or co-worker problem. Instead, his personal insecurities caused him to see things that weren't there and hear things that weren't said.

Jason's response to this situation is not uncommon. He was about to start a new relationship with another job and more than likely repeat a cycle. Let me show you what the engagement cycle looks like in an unhealthy and a healthy way.

UNHEALTHY CYCLE OF ENGAGEMENT

Step 1 - Honeymoon:
The relationship is great! You are so excited as this is a God send and you have never experienced anything like this in life!

Step 2 - Engage:
You start to engage in the relationship and interact in ways that allow you to see some areas that need improvement, but you still go full steam ahead. You use words like "we" and "us"

Step 3 - Conflict:
You encounter some unexpected things in the other person, and it starts to ruin your dream (selfishness, controlling nature, etc). These things trigger things inside of you and the honeymoon ends. You may feel overlooked, experience rejection, or you encounter resistance to your ideas and thoughts from the other person.

Step 4 - Response:
You either quit, pull away and withdraw, only giving suggestions, get bitter, start fighting, start discerning evil spirits, or lose hope. You start to think, "I don't need this to define me. I have other options." You also start the process of generalization. You get critical of everything. You begin to form relationship with people who have the same problems as you in relationships. You fail to confront the appropriate parties you have challenges with and you just discuss your problems but you never address the problems.

Step 5 - Repeat:
You move on with new relationship, but with unresolved issues from your past relationship. You don't realize it but you enter the new relationship mad, frustrated, hurt, unfulfilled, over-eager, naive, with unrealistic expectations, or no expectations at all because you didn't engage properly in the last relationship. So you keep trying to get it right in new ones.

HEALTHY CYCLE OF ENGAGEMENT

Step 1 - Honeymoon:
The relationship is great! You are so excited as this is a God send and you have never experienced anything like this in life! Embrace this moment and look to establish heart-to-heart connections!

Step 6 - Growth:
You strengthen your current relationship (or transition out of it if the season is over) with no hard feelings. You are open and ready for new relationships because you know how to engage and interact.

Step 2 - Engage:
You start to engage in the relationship and interact in ways that allow you to see some areas that need improvement, but you still go full steam ahead. You use words like "we" and "us"

Step 5 - Results:
Benefits, Benefits, Benefits! Personal growth and relationship growth.

Step 3 - Conflict:
You encounter some unexpected things in the other person, and it starts to ruin your dream (selfishness, controlling nature, etc). These things trigger things inside of you and the honeymoon ends. You may feel overlooked, experience rejection, or you encounter resistance to your ideas and thoughts from the other person. At this point you should seek God for clarity. Find the source of the conflict by doing a heart check: pride, ego, offense, bitterness. Ask yourself what role am I playing in the problem and what role can I play in the solution?

Step 4 - Response:
Don't take conflict personal. Express your concern and add additional counsel if the other person isn't hearing you. Do not quit. Develop a solution and work it. Find a way to make things work by focusing on the overall goal. Don't withdraw. Engage in heart-to-heart talks. Pray!

I have found that seeing the cycle of engagement illustrated in a healthy and unhealthy way is very helpful.

A Guide to Identifying Engagement Problems

If you're still not sure the best way to engage with others to solve relationship problems, I recommend reviewing the 5 Cs: care, communication, chemistry and compatibility, and control.

Care: Caring is like the heart which is pumping life into the relationship. People care because they have love for the relationship and for the parties involved in the relationship. Some people get to a point where they are just heartless and couldn't care less about the relationships they are in. When you feel this way, you will dishonor and disrespect those with whom you are in relationship.

When you don't care, you won't check yourself when you are selfish or being prideful. People who don't care disregard others' feelings and they bully others into doing things their way. Sometimes, it is easy to physically stay in a relationship that you mentally, emotionally, and spiritually have already checked out of.

In contrast, when you care, you pay attention to the people you are connected to. You pick up on things about the other person and you can respond to them in a loving way. You notice the smallest details about those you are connected to. You know what situations they thrive in, you know when (and when not) to deliver information to them, you can pick up on their moods, you know what makes them tick and what shuts them down, and you know when to call or text to check them. This list could go on and on as caring is one of the greatest keys to a lasting relationship.

Q&A Checkpoint: Ask yourself

- Am I operating with a caring heart?

Communication: When you do not care, your communication will also suffer. The Bible says, "out of the abundance of the heart the mouth speaks." Your communication displays what your heart believes. Consider this: if caring is the heart of the relationship, then communication is the brain of the relationship. When you have communication problems, this is like a relationship being brain dead or having little brain activity. There are no signals coming from the brain to trigger any activity in the body to get anything done in the relationship.

Communication must flow for relationships to see benefits. Communication is a two-way street. It requires speaking, listening, being in the moment, being engaged, and working towards an end. Engagement problems happen in relationships when there are communication problems. When this happens, the relationship will go stale and have a good chance of dying because there is no life flowing in the relationship.

One-sided communication is also a problem. People who are self-absorbed only talk about themselves and only see the world through their own eyes. They will find themselves frustrated in relationships because eventually the people they relate to have nothing to say.

In other instances, communication within the relationship is non-existent. People shut down and refuse to talk for various reasons. No one can read your mind. You must actually, *say* how you feel as opposed to *projecting* how you feel. Don't get mad if the other person does not automatically know how you feel. A good relationship is not measured by expecting the other person to be a psychic.

Communication is also a challenge when people do not watch their tone. *How* you communicate is just as important as *what* you communicate. Your tone can discredit your message. Tone can be how your message is verbally stated – the volume of your voice, traces of sarcasm, etc. – as well as body language while you are communicating.

If people frequently tell you that you should watch the way you say things, but you don't think you are communicating anything wrong, then you need to ask yourself, "what do I believe about the person I am in relationship with?" For instance, if you think people are stupid, your tone could be condescending.

This last communication challenge that I want to discuss is when people fail to set boundaries with their words. You will fight in relationships, but you must learn how to fight fair. "Fight" doesn't mean you try to kill each other; it simply means you learn how to disagree. You can't call people names, insult their family members or attack their personal attributes, and expect benefits to show up in your relationships. You must learn to master your emotions and carefully choose words regardless of how you feel when you are communicating your message.

 **Checkpoint. Ask yourself**

- Do I communicate well in my relationships?

- Do my tone and body language suggest I am open to a two-sided conversation?

- Do I listen well when the other person shares his or her personal thoughts and feelings?

- Do I fight fair?

Chemistry and Compatibility: Chemistry and compatibility is fun to watch and experience. Like when Kool-Aid meets sugar, cheese meets cake, fire meets a marinated steak, or Michael Jordan meets Scottie Pippen... chemistry happens and ignites a flame of passion inside of each person in the relationship.

When people have chemistry and compatibility, they know each other, they can finish each other's sentences, they know each other's strengths, weakness and hot buttons, and they simply just "click" and fit together. They are going in the same direction.

This happens not because one person makes changes to accommodate the other's desires. But it happens when two people know who they are individually, find their path in life independently and then they find each other on the same path.

This is true for romance, work, church, business, or any place a relationship is born.

When there is no chemistry you don't flow well together. You will be classic underachievers and under-performers. It will feel like you are wasting your time because you are putting a lot of effort into a relationship and seeing no results. You will feel like you are working against each other. Guess what: you are right. You are. You aren't connected.

A lack of chemistry is painful. There is just no spark; there's nothing. I have found that a lack of compatibility is often not personal, rather it happens as a result of growth and the paths we take in life. It's simply not having common ground with a person or perhaps just being on different paths. Sometimes people simply grow apart.

A lack of compatibility exists when there are two people with visions and paths that do not merge. A lack of compatibility cannot be fixed by more engagement and interaction. As a matter of fact, it may be worsened by more fellowship. Let's face it: every relationship is not meant to last.

Q&A Checkpoint: Ask yourself

- Are my relationships suffering due to a lack of chemistry?

- Am I holding on to an outdated version of someone that no longer exists? (What I call an assumed closeness or familiarity where you thought you knew someone, but they've since changed and evolved into a whole new person.)

- Is it me? It is very easy to assume it's the other party when you are having challenges. I get frustrated with the talk-to-text function on my smartphone. One day I was planning to contact the phone manufacturer and complain. Then it hit me to ask my son to say what I was trying to say into my phone. Would you believe that it worked perfectly for him? The only thing wrong with my talk-to-text function was the "nut" loose holding the phone. Me! Before you assess the relationship, ask yourself, "is it me?"

Control: When there is no care, bad communication and little or no chemistry in a relationship, many people try to control the other person to produce benefits. When you try to control the relationship, you will manipulate or use any means to produce the image of a relationship that you see in your head. This is not healthy, and it is not natural. It may look good on social media and convey a positive external image to the outsider looking in, but internally it is dysfunctional.

 **Checkpoint:**

- Am I controlling?

- Do I trust my counterpart's judgement enough to give them freedom in decision-making? Trust is the ability to focus on one's tasks while letting others focus on theirs, thus optimizing efforts. Equally, trust also allows for team members to check up on each other to make sure all tasks remain aligned with the common goal.

- Am I snooping and double-checking? Do I go behind them and do it my way?

Fix Engagement Problems in Three Steps

#1: Check back in! You have to start caring again. Caring brings intimacy back to the relationship. When you check back in, your heart comes back alive and as a result of caring you will start to plan together. You will think and operate with the mindset of what is best for the relationship not just me as a person. You study the people that you are connected with to get to know them.

You may be asking, "how do I check back in?" It is simple but challenging. You decide to care again, and all of your actions, thoughts, emotions, and conversations have to be aligned to reflect that decision. For instance, when you don't care, you don't listen. Checking back in means, you decide to listen versus blocking out everything a person says when they talk. You make your heart open to feel again.

Caring makes you vulnerable to be hurt and disappointed. This is scary for many people because the reason you stopped caring was because you were hurt and disappointed. However, think about this; if you don't

28

open back up, then you will never experience the love and fulfillment that could possibly come through the relationship. Pray and listen to the Holy Spirit as to how to move forward.

#2: Own the gaps. If you feel disconnected in your relationship you should be assertive and own the gap. The gap is the disconnect you feel. Normally we tell ourselves when there are gaps that if the other person cared, then "they would reach out to me," "they would call or text me," etc. Here's what I have discovered; sometimes you have to take the initiative and start the conversation.

When there are gaps in relationships, there is normally no communication or bad communication. Take the time to fill the gaps and reconnect at the heart with the person, people, or organization you are a part of.

Revisit your why, deal with your personal feelings, and decide, "do I value why we are together over what is currently going on enough to reconnect

I once had a person come to me who felt like we had grown apart. I pastor a church and my friend felt that as the church had grown, he was out of the loop, I didn't talk to him as much and he felt as if I valued other people over his loyalty and commitment.

I had no clue he felt this way. He waited a long time to tell me and by the time he did, a lot of things had built up in his mind, and a lot of things that I did fed into his assumptions. When we finally talked, he was upset that is took so long to actually talk and why I didn't sense the disconnect.

I felt horrible. Not making excuses, but I had so many things on me. The Holy Spirit spoke to me in that moment and I asked this person why he didn't come to me when he first felt this as opposed to waiting.

"How could you not know?" he responded to me.

It was awkward but I said, "Since you were the one who had the feeling, that was the Holy Spirit leading you and guiding you to the idea that we needed to talk; not the beginning of a standoff."

When you love someone -regardless of your position- you make a decision to own the gap, make adjustments, and make an attempt to fix the disconnect. When you allow time to continue with a disconnect, sometimes horrible things will be assumed that are not true, and small things can balloon into big issues.

As you are reading this, I am sure you have felt this way with many people. Fall on the side of love and send that text, make that call, or connect with them on social media. Own your feelings, seize the opportunity to initiate contact and own the gap to reconnect.

#3: Trust. Trust is not verbal, it is behavioral. When you do not trust people, you will more than likely exhibit control issues. I believe at the end of the day people try to control things not because they are malicious people but because they don't want to be hurt. This results in a lack of boundaries because you can't control every aspect of a relationship.

Here is something to consider when building trust. Learn a person's judgment. You must give people the room to make decisions and you should monitor how they make decisions to determine the level of influence you give them in your life. To start building trust, give someone small amounts of influence in your life (and you don't even have to announce that you are doing this). Observe how the person handles this influence as you increase levels of trust in him or her. Always remember forgiving someone doesn't equal reconciliation or restored trust. Restored trust and reconciliation are different steps that happen over time.

Relationships produce benefits at the speed of trust. Have you ever had to complete a task with someone, and it took you forever? Not because the task was hard but because your counterpart didn't trust you or the situation. When you don't trust a person, you aren't saying necessarily that a person can't do something. You are saying, "I don't believe that person will do it - whether they can or not!" Our ability to trust is shaped by what we experienced or what others close to us have experienced! In order to be social-ish and have our relationships produce benefits, you must know how to trust. I am going to give you principles on how to build trust.

- *Choose to be trustworthy* - Choosing to be trustworthy doesn't mean you are flawless. You are worthy of trust when you can admit to your flaws and mistakes. I know I am flawed, but I am trusting the Holy Spirit to cause me to address things in my life and I am going to trust God to do the same to those around me. Sometimes we have a mistrust for people not for what they have done but from our guilt causing us to be paranoid. If you look at businesses and how investors choose to invest, they invest in the person and not necessarily a person's idea. They want to know, "will they win? Will they admit when they are wrong? Will they respond well to failure? Will they listen and learn?" Choosing to be trustworthy is the first step in developing trust.

- *Build your circle with trustworthy people* - Proverbs 13:20 says, "He who walks with wise men will be wise, But the companion of fools will suffer harm." Whatever you are around consistently you will become. There is a statement I read once that I love and live by. It says, "show me your friends and I will show you your future!" We should be on a constant search to find trustworthy people. When you find trustworthy people, remember they are not perfect, they are guided by principles that make them feel safe. Spend time with these people to develop trust and resist the urge to pull away when things may alarm you. Remember, you build your trust in someone by spending time with something on someone not by staying away!

- *Pray for wisdom on how to trust* - We focus on "who" should I trust, when I think the right thing, we should focus on is "how" should I trust. My son is 12 years old. I love him but, I don't trust him with my wife's and my money. He is not mature enough to handle it. If given the opportunity, he would spend all our money and we couldn't take care of our responsibilities. Trust works the same way. Study a person to figure out his level of maturity, humility and wisdom, and then determine what level of trust can you give him.

We tend to go in extremes. We either trust people or we don't. This is how you can let people earn trust without even saying it. Watch how they handle your heart, things you tell them, and how they respond when you ask them to do things. Over time you will learn to pull back, go all in, or simply cut people off. Trust is a choice not something that is demanded. It is something you confidently give or take from people or situations. Using trust this way will cause you to produce benefits and not be manipulated or hurt as you are being social-ish.

Q&A Check Your Engagement Pulse

Another great way to discover if you're having engagement problems is to ask people you are in relationship with the following questions. Listen to the responses completely and take in the answers without debating. Repeat back to the person what you hear them saying about you!

- Do I blame others for my personal dissatisfaction, or do I own what I feel is missing in the relationship? Give me a specific example

- Do I act like I care? Give me examples that show I care and those that do show I don't.

- Am I self-aware? Remember the statement people with problems get in relationships and they blame the relationship for their personal problems? Relationships help expose your need for personal maturity. Embrace it and let the other person help you.

Accept When Relationships Are Over

Shifts, transitions and sometimes the dismantling of relationships are a natural part of life. Children leave their parents' house. Employees move to different jobs. Families find new church homes. Friends develop new lives in different social circles. And unfortunately, some relationships even become toxic and abusive.

People are in your life for a season, some for a reason, and some for a lifetime; the test of time will prove which category each person belongs in. This is why I believe relationships don't have to end badly.

People pick different paths based on their purpose and sometimes this causes the dynamics of your relationship to change. When you grow apart, it doesn't make either of you bad people it just makes you different. The challenge in relationships is when people have to stay stuck in an era or place in their life in order to stay connected to another person or group of people. I see this dynamic all the time and people end up very frustrated and miserable with themselves and at some point, regret and resentment set in and they blame others for their lack of growth.

People in this situation delay progression in life trying to "save relationships." Relationships are all about giving each other the space to mature and find yourself. I grew up with a set of guys that I am still close to in my adult life. Growing up, I couldn't imagine us ever not talking every day or not being in the same place. However, there was a time in our lives when I moved away and took a separate path from them. As a matter of fact, we all did. I didn't see them every day and we didn't talk much at all. When we did see each other, it was like we picked up right where we left off. We all had separate paths to go down, we made other friendships and moved on in life.

Ironically, all of us live in the same area now, but we didn't do that so we could be friends. Our paths in life brought us back together. I believe a great challenge in relationships is when people don't understand their paths and they stay stuck in a place to try to hold onto a relationship. People do this while dating, with family, on the job, at church, etc. You must follow where God is leading you and you will have incredible relationships with people who are going in the same direction you are going in.

It is a miserable state in life trying to relate to someone or even a place that you are not going in the same direction as and you have different interests and values. But as long as your heart is in the right place, it's ok to embrace the natural shift away from one another. It doesn't make either of you evil, it just means you're not compatible and you have to evaluate your closeness as seasons of your life change.

 **Checkpoint:**

- Is this a relationship I should have in this season of my life?

- Are we going in the same direction and do we have the same beliefs, values and interests?

social·*ish*

CHAPTER 3

How to ensure benefits in relationships?

If benefits from relationships are not showing up in your life, you should ask yourself, "am I allowing myself to be provoked in relationships," or "am I provoking others to good works in my relationships?"

The Bible says that we should provoke one another to good works. To provoke means to stimulate, sometimes irritate, and push to do great things. We need people to pull things out of us that we can't see in ourselves and to challenge things in us that we can't see in ourselves. To get maximum benefits, I believe there are three types of engagement that are needed in a relationship. I call it three types of provoking.

Embrace Encouragers

Encouraging is this type of engagement that calls out your potential. This provoking pulls on the best in you. It causes you to dream beyond where you are. It builds and stirs your faith to imagine what you could do and what could be done in any situation.

I have several encouragers in my life. They always send an encouraging text at the right time and it is normally out of the blue. They believe in me no matter what. They see things in me that I don't see in myself. They push me to

levels I never thought possible and pull things out of me
that I wanted to do but didn't believe that I could.

Encouraging is good because it places a demand on your
potential. The only problem is everybody comes with a gift
and an issue. Encouragers normally don't address your
issues; they just address your potential.

Seek Out Challengers

Challenging is this type of engaging that challenges your
potential. I call this type of provoking a reality check.

For every dream and goal that you have, challengers ask
you a lot of questions to make sure you have your bases
covered. Challenging must be done in love because if not
it will be seen as an attack.

Challengers make sure you see things from every angle.
They are the mirrors we need to help us see our errors.
Often times our emotions and thoughts only allow us to
see a limited view of every situation. Challengers cause
you to see things from more than your perspective.
Challengers are not looking to be on your side; they are on
the side of what is best.

The right relationships, when you trust them, can show
you things about yourself that help you reach your full
potential. All the "help" you get may not feel good to you,
but it is good *for* you.

Proverbs 27:6 states, "Faithful are the wounds of a friend,
but deceitful are the kisses of an enemy." A sign of a true
friend is that he or she is willing to "wound" with words that
we need to hear but many are afraid to tell us out of fear
of losing our friendship, being deemed a hater, or hurting

us. These "wounds" are necessary to heal and restore us as much as we need encouragement in love. But they may not feel good.

In some instances, the people around you only tell you what they want you to hear to flatter you, but they leave certain feedback out that you need to hear. When I was in graduate school, one of my instructors observed that I was a good public speaker. He frequently asked me to speak in front of the class. But I began to notice that my classmates didn't respond or "respect" me like I thought they should. Finally, my friend finally told me, "Jason, you are just loud and come across as confident, but we all know that you don't read and study your content the way you should. You can't just emotionally connect in this setting like you do at church."

The feedback from my friend hurt my feelings, and I was embarrassed. However, I knew what she told me was true. So, I made the adjustments and it helped tremendously. I wanted to be better and self-awareness allowed me to do that.

This type of provoking is missing in many people's lives. No one is allowed to challenge stories, emotions, and decisions and a lot of assumption are made because the complaints are just heard by encouragers. Encouragers many times do not address conflict.

Challenging is uncomfortable but good in that you can dream and address reality at the same time. It forces you to deal with your issues. When you realize its purpose, you understand it isn't ruining your dreams. Instead, it addresses the issues that could cause your dreams to be nightmares and provides a mechanism for healthy course correction.

Select an Accountability Partner

Accountability is needed in your life because it is the bridge that helps close the gap between encouraging (potential) and challenging (reality). Accountability is essentially the guardian of your potential as you pursue your dreams.

An accountability partner helps you to develop into the best version of yourself. Accountability partners don't judge you for being the person who you are today. Much like a trainer at the gym, those who hold you accountable should use words that are full of life, not have a demeaning tone or shaming you for your current state. But they are right by your side to help you stay on the right path and make you better.

We can all help each other get better without belittling each other. Being social-ish is all about helping each other to be better so that we can be better together.

I believe when those three elements of encouraging, challenging, and accountability are in place, benefits can't help but to show up in your life. I want to challenge you to make a list of the following:

- Who are the encouragers in my life?
- Who are my challengers, and do I allow them the right to challenge me?
- Who is holding me accountable in my life?
- Who am I encouraging?
- Who am I challenging?
- Who am I holding accountable?

CHAPTER 4

Be social·*ish* *everyday*

I believe that in order for the information shared in the previous chapters to be relevant, you must first know yourself. It is important to know who you are as a person before you can connect with other people.

Social-ish people are first social-ish with themselves. You may be wondering *how can I be social-ish with myself?* Easy! It is called having an identity. We see other people through the lens by which we see ourselves. If you don't have a healthy view of yourself, you will have a distorted view of others. You can either see them for more than what they are and set yourself up for a letdown, or not see them for all that they are and miss out on the full benefits they bring into your life.

Learning To Love Myself So I Can Love Others

In the Bible, Jesus was asked what the greatest command-ments were. I love His response. He said love the Lord your God with your whole being and love your neighbor as yourself. Then he said, **"Do this and you will live."**

I believe one of the most overlooked parts of His statement is "love your neighbor as yourself." We understand we should love God with everything we have. However, I want to propose something to you. We live in a time when people are not authentically themselves. I think it is a shame to be born an original but die a copy of someone or something you chose to be instead of being yourself. This scripture says, "love your neighbor as yourself." You must love your neighbor as **you**, not as who you pretend to be. God wants to bless who He created you to be, not who you pretend to be.

The challenge is in relationships, sometimes we pretend to be a lot of things and we become a lot of things just to be in a relationship. The pressure of a relationship causes us to compromise our character and integrity, or we turn into a toxic version of ourselves as a result of trying to keep the wrong person in our lives. We all should discover who we are and then we can be good at relationships.

As a result of discovering our identity, we can effectively love others. We discover who we are through a relationship with the Lord. When we love our neighbor as ourselves, the Bible says we will live.

A lot of people are alive but not really living. I lived in a city that I hated at one point in my life. However, something happened when I started to come into my own, discover my identity and be confident with myself. It brought me into a different circle of people. These people showed me a side of this city that I had never seen. I found restaurants I didn't know existed. They taught me the history of the city. I found cool places to hang out, took great walks, and best of all I met people who brought me out of my sell and tremendously impacted my life.

Loving my neighbors as myself has awakened a side of life I never imagined. I had to accept my personality, my learning style, my calling, and everything that comes with me. The more I refine who I am, the better I am in relationships. I believe one of the greatest gifts you can give people is the gift of self-improvement. A great deal of people blame relationship problems or problems in general on other people. I suggest looking in the mirror first. When you know who you are, you can look in the mirror and adjust yourself to be social-ish in any context you find yourself in.

Are you loving people as yourself or a modified version of you? Spend some time with yourself and learn who you are.

You may be asking yourself, "how do I learn who I am? How do I come to understand the intricacies and nuances of my personality?" Here are some questions that I feel will help you get to know yourself:

- Do you know your personality type? Go take a personality test to help you discover great things about yourself.

- What insecurities or opportunities for growth in your personality have you accepted and called it "my personality?"

  Let me give you an example. I have had several opportunities to go into sales. However, I always told myself that sales is not "my personality. I can name numerous occasions when I was approached for sales positions and the industry has always appealed to me. One day I had to be honest with myself, with the help of a challenger (see previous chapter). I could have been a great salesman I just didn't like the pressure and had a fear of failing. Then in 2009, with the help of a team, I started a church from scratch. Take a wild guess what skills I needed: the ability to sale and approach people. I would have been better prepared to walk in my calling had I taken previous opportunities to prepare myself that I talked myself out of because I really wasn't "good" at being social-ish.

- In what types of situations do you find it hard to be social-ish and why?

  I used to shut down socially when it came to doing presentations in my former jobs. I am comfortable preaching in a church but presenting from overhead slideshows always made me nervous. My brain wouldn't function well, my voice would shake, and I would shutter at answering questions even though I had the answers. One day, I finally admitted to someone I had a fear of looking stupid and being asked a question I didn't know the answer to.

  I thought I had a fear problem that stopped me from being social-ish. It was not fear; it was pride. I noticed I was fine if I thought I was smarter or as smart as everyone in the room. However, if I perceived that someone in the room was smarter, more accomplished, or generally more qualified than me, I would retreat into a shell. That's not fear; that is pride. I wanted to be better than everyone instead of making the room I was in better. Once I learned this, I was able to adjust and be social-ish in uncomfortable situations.

- What types of situations cause you to feel alive and make it is easy to be social-ish?

  I feel alive in environments with driven people who are well versed on what they do but they value the concept of team and making the people around them better. Why is this? Because I recharge alone, as most introverts do, but I grow, learn, and excel in the setting of a great team. I love a challenge. I love being challenged. I love playing and winning together. Losing is even tolerable if I know we gave all we had as a team.

Once you have a good grasp of yourself you can begin to see people for who they really are and not what you want them to be. Once you have seen who they are, your social-ish skills can kick in and you can engage appropriately. Once you set the expectation of who this person is and what you are going to give and receive from them, you will be surprised at what opens up in life through being social-ish. Here's the lynchpin to being social-ish: you must determine who and how a person relates to you in order to receive benefits from the relationship. And who the person is determines how you will engage with them!

social·*ish*

Conclusion

Congratulations! You have made it to the end of the book. I pray that you found the information in this book useful. I am no relationship expert, but my desire is to share relationship principles to help you become social-ish and get the most out of the relationships in your life. These principles work for me and for countless others that I have taught them to.

I think one of the greatest tragedies in life is to be surrounded by great people and never see the full benefit of what is possible when God brings us together. Let's be honest. Our world, country, and even our communities face constant tension in relationships. We face things that divide us racially, religiously, economically or just personal preferences that place us at odds. The barriers between us are real and should not be ignored. But I believe many – if not all barriers between us – can be overcome and we can be social-ish with each other by using the principles in this book.

I want you to stop and think about this statement. The relationships in your life that have the greatest potential for benefits (to the world and your personal life) will be challenged the most. I believe we face a real enemy which is not walking around in flesh and blood. This enemy rather plants things in the hearts and minds of people trying to get them to think and believe things that are not true. These lies form the basis of what stops us from being social-ish.

As you approach your relationships each day, I want to you to think, "how can I connect with people where I am, and why does God have me here?" If you are having problems, then ask yourself – based on what you have learned – am I having relationship problems or engaging problems? Once you determine that, take the proper course of action and go be as social-ish as you can.

I want you to see so many benefits showing up in your life that you look every obstacle that comes your and say, "I will be social-ish and I will see the God-ordained benefits of every relationship in my life!"

ABOUT THE
Author

Jason D. Scales is a native of Shelbyville, TN. He currently resides in Murfreesboro, TN. He is the husband of Barbara A. Scales and the proud father of Isaiah Scales. Jason pastors the Believers Faith Fellowship Church in Christiana, TN. He earned a B.S. in Psychology and MBA at the University of Tennessee at Chattanooga.

Jason also has two other books that you may enjoy. They both can be purchased on Amazon.com.

Resilient: How to Bounce Back from Loss!

The harsh reality of losing things is not one that we often train ourselves to handle. We seek prosperity, but it is rare that we discuss how to endure in the face of adversity. Being people of faith does not exempt us from loss and setbacks. This book teaches how to tap into your resilience and emerge from loss victoriously. You may have lost a few battles, but the war can still be won. Sometimes, we never see the promises of God because we die before we stop breathing. No matter what you endure, don't die in the place of your affliction!

How's That Working for You?

How's that working for you?" is a phrase designed to help you take a lighthearted or perhaps comical look at things that aren't working in your life? This book describes fictional stories based on real life experiences people encounter every day in hopes that you will see yourself or someone you know in the story. As a result of reading this book I want you to be able to determine what isn't working and to find what does work in life!

Stay Connected

Jason would like to connect with you! Below are a few ways you can connect with Jason, stay updated on new releases, and get information on upcoming events!

Facebook: Jason Scales

Instagram: @jscales3

Email: jscales3@yahoo.com

social·ish

A FAIL PROOF GUIDE TO RELATIONSHIPS

jason scales

Made in the USA
Coppell, TX
16 May 2020

25713667R00039